Wednesfield and Heath Town

IN OLD PHOTOGRAPHS

Wednesfield and Heath Town

IN OLD PHOTOGRAPHS

Collected by ELIZABETH REES
and MARY MILLS

Alan Sutton Publishing Limited
Phoenix Mill · Far Thrupp
Stroud · Gloucestershire

ALAN
SUTTON

First published 1992

Front Cover Illustration:
Wednesfield Road around 1900.

**British Library Cataloguing
in Publication Data**

Rees, Elizabeth
 Wednesfield and Heath Town in Old
 Photographs
 I. Title II. Mills, Mary
 942.46

 ISBN 0–7509–0133–0

Typeset in 9/10 Sabon.
Typesetting and origination by
Alan Sutton Publishing Limited.
Printed and bound by
WBC, Bridgend, Mid Glam.

Contents

Done's Bakery in 1900 and 1983, one of the oldest established businesses in Wednesfield.

Introduction

The area covered by the photographs in this book is part of the present borough of Wolverhampton and lies to the north east of the town centre. It is enclosed by Park Lane and Cannock Road to the west, the borough boundary to the north and east, and the Willenhall Road to the south. Wednesfield Road, Wolverhampton Road and Lichfield Road form the main artery through the area. Wednesfield, Heath Town (formerly known as Wednesfield Heath), Park Village and Fallings Park formed the ancient Liberty of Wednesfield, later Wednesfield parish, while Springfield was in the parish of Wolverhampton.

The earliest mention of Wednesfield occurs in the Anglo-Saxon Chronicle for 910 which states that a battle took place there between the Saxons, under Edward the Elder, and the Danes. The actual location of the battle, although marked on maps at Bowmans Harbour, is very doubtful, but it is clear that the name is of pagan Saxon origin, derived from the god Woden.

In 994 Wednesfield formed part of the land given by Wulfrun to the church at Hamtun, which afterwards became Wulfrun's Hamtun, or Wolverhampton. Many of the boundaries mentioned in the charter laid the basis for the later boundaries of Wednesfield parish.

By the Domesday survey of 1086 Wednesfield belonged to the canons of Wolverhampton. There were six villeins and six bordars with six ploughs and woodland for pannage, which may indicate a total population of about sixty, scattered throughout the parish. A distinctive feature of the area in mediaeval and early modern times was the large number of moated settlements, such as Moathouse and Ashmore Park, many of which could still be seen until comparatively recently, and the names of which have been preserved in those of local housing estates. Among the families who lived in these farmsteads were the Levesons, the Hopes, the Goughs and the Perrys.

The Liberty of Wednesfield remained very small until the mid-eighteenth century, when the beginnings of industry and the coming of the canals attracted more people to the area. This growth was marked by the fact that Wednesfield acquired its own church and subsequently became a parish in its own right. Industrially, the area was similar to Wolverhampton and the Black Country, with coal mining and iron-related trades predominating. Locks, keys and traps were especially typical products of small-scale industry in Wednesfield, while larger factories gradually appeared, particularly in Heath Town. The population grew from 1,088 in 1801 to 8,553 in 1861. By 1891, when separate figures were quoted for Wednesfield and Heath Town, Wednesfield had a population of 4,949, while Heath Town housed 7,075.

Kelly's Directory for 1896 lists the 'manufactures' of Heath Town as 'hydraulic pumps, safes, bucket ears, washers, locks, keys, traps, latches, hinges, shovels and bicycles, tin trunks, bonnet boxes and iron'. The same directory also gives a vivid description of the area as seen from the banks of the canal: 'On the south west a commanding view is afforded of the eastern side of the town of Wolverhampton; on the south east the numerous blast furnaces and coal and ironstone pits present at night a grand and striking scene.'

A Sanitary Committee for Wednesfield and Heath Town was set up in 1856, becoming a Local Board in 1863. In 1866 Heath Town set up its own Local Board and the two subsequently went their own way, both becoming Urban District Councils in 1894. Heath Town quickly became swallowed up by Wolverhampton and in 1927 the Heath Town Urban District ceased to exist. Wednesfield, however, remained entirely independent and physically separate until the early 1950s when Wolverhampton's overspill housing policy began and new estates were built there. The Urban District was absorbed into Wolverhampton in 1966 despite much local opposition. The overspill agreement marked a complete turning point for Wednesfield. In 1951 only 2,000 people lived in the overspill area, 90 per cent in Wood End village, whereas by 1971 over 19,000 lived there, of whom only 10 per cent lived in Wood End.

The twentieth-century development of this area has been essentially one of increasing urbanization and this is reflected in the collection of photographs in this book. Heath Town was the first area to become urbanized as long rows of terraced houses, many with others in courts behind, were built in the nineteenth century. The area suffered from problems of public health from that time, but it was not until the 1960s that the last of the old terraces were demolished to make way for the blocks of flats which are the distinctive feature of the area today, and which have brought their own problems with them.

Springfield was developed in the nineteenth century as part of Wolverhampton's earliest town planning, but this too was unsuccessful and virtually all the houses built at that time have since disappeared. Park Village, as a separate area, first appears around the turn of the century when private housing development began to fill in what had previously been open land. The housing in this area remains virtually unchanged, with only the local industries having grown up, flourished and gone, to make way for others, some in the old factory premises and others in new industrial units. Fallings Park is most interesting, as an example of town planning under the garden suburb movement which grew up at the turn of the century in a reaction against the rows of terraced housing which had been thrown up by speculative builders. The idea was to give workers airy houses surrounded by open spaces which they could enjoy communally, and the application of some of this philosophy can still be seen in the area. However, the scheme was never entirely finished and many of the open spaces have since been filled in with further housing development.

Ironically for the historic centre of the area, Wednesfield waited until last for urban development, the area remaining comparatively rural until the 1950s. Wednesfield village, too, lacked the amenities expected of a central focus until the influx of people demanded facilities such as a market and increased numbers and variety of shops.

The photographs in this collection have been chosen to reflect the development of the area as a whole, while showing the contrasts between the component parts, many of which have changed beyond recognition. The surviving landmarks that can be seen in the pictures highlight the sweeping changes that have taken place throughout the area.

SECTION ONE

Wednesfield

Wednesfield High Street in the early 1950s. In a Board of Health report of 1848, Wednesfield is described as 'a town or village consisting principally of one street', and this street was the High Street.

High Street in the early 1960s. This photograph shows how congested this street was before widening. For many years the trolleybus service from Wolverhampton was forced to terminate at the Dog and Partridge because the bridge was too narrow for the buses.

High Street in 1959. This shows clearly how the road widening took place with the new buildings constructed behind the old ones which were then demolished. The old post office can be seen on the left.

High Street looking towards Church Street in the early 1960s. St Thomas' church is on the left of the picture.

The site of Barclays Bank, High Street in 1955.

Church Street Canal Bridge in 1970, looking towards Graiseley Lane.

Well Lane in 1959 looking towards St Thomas' church. This scene looks quite different today as all of the old buildings have been demolished.

Cross Street, Wednesfield, which was completely obliterated by the Hickman Estate of high rise flats in the 1970s. The photograph was taken in 1959.

The back of Rookery Street in the 1930s. Back yards such as these were communally used for outhouses, toilets, or hanging out washing, and also sometimes had communal taps or pumps.

Graiseley Lane in the 1930s looking towards St Thomas' church.

Orchard Buildings, Graiseley Lane in 1955. These were typical local houses with workshops at the back where the local industries such as lock and key making were carried on.

Rickyard Buildings in 1939. These houses were at the end of Church Street and the beginning of High Street and were demolished when the bank was built.

Neachells Farm in about 1950. This house belonged to Silvester Hayes in the early 1600s, and later to the Grosvenor family. Originally moated, it was destroyed during coal mining in the late nineteenth century.

Wolverhampton Road at the junction with New Street, looking back towards New Cross. The building on the left was the tram terminus.

The Wyrley and Essington Canal from Pinfold Bridge in about 1952. This canal, opened in 1795, is supposed to be the highest in England, and was first built to carry coal from Wyrley and Essington to Wolverhampton and Walsall. Later extensions carried the Midland canal system to Cannock Chase when large-scale coal mining began in that area. It was popularly known as the 'Curly Wyrley' because of its winding nature.

The Wyrley and Essington Canal in about 1920, showing how some of the houses actually looked on to the canal rather than a street or court.

St Thomas' church, built by voluntary subscription and consecrated in 1750. Wednesfield had originally been part of the parish of Wolverhampton, but an Act of 1741 allowed a church to be built there on the grounds that the 'mother church of Wolverhampton aforesaid is near two miles distant from Wednesfield aforesaid and the highway or road between Wednesfield aforesaid and the said church being very deep and dirty in the winter season'.

Two views of the interior of the old St Thomas' church, one looking towards the altar and the other towards the back of the church. The body of the original church was extensively altered in the 1840s and again in 1884. These photographs appear to date from between these two alterations.

St Thomas' church after the fire of 18 January 1902 which destroyed most of the building except for the shell of the nave and the tower. Wolverhampton Fire Brigade apparently took half an hour to reach Wednesfield as they had to make several stops to rest their horses on the way. The Willenhall brigade was unable to attend at all as it could not obtain any horses. In the photograph a group of parishioners surveys the damage.

Another view of St Thomas' church after the fire. This picture clearly shows the destruction of the gallery which can be seen on p. 22, as well as the fact that the whole of the roof had been destroyed.

An early view of the rebuilt St Thomas' church, showing the remains of the original tower topped with new work, and the changed line of the roof. The photograph also shows Church Bridge, and the small house with its workshop attached where keys were made on the site of the present library.

St Thomas' church from the south, with the wall of Wednesfield House on the right. Some of the cottages on the left still stand today, virtually all that remains of the old village.

A similar view in the 1950s, showing the rebuilt church more clearly. The height of the churchyard wall has been reduced and the trees severely pruned.

Two interior views of the church following the rebuilding. The first dates from
before 1918 when the rood beam, which
can be clearly seen in the lower photograph, was erected as a memorial to the
123 Wednesfield men who were killed in
the First World War.

The old Wednesfield Vicarage, Prestwood Road West. Vicarage Road was constructed to form a convenient route for the vicar from his home to the church via Graiseley Lane.

Revd John Birch, vicar of Wednesfield from 1881 to 1915, and Mrs Birch outside the vicarage.

Wednesfield Trinity Methodist church, which was dedicated on 17 March 1887, was opened to replace the old Rookery Street chapel which had become too small. In 1964 it absorbed the congregation of Hickman Street church, but the amalgamated Wednesfield Methodist church moved to Wood End in 1983 and Trinity was demolished soon afterwards.

Hickman Street Methodist chapel was originally built in 1850 to house the Primitive Methodists who had been meeting in a cottage in Lichfield Road. The chapel in the photograph was built in 1885 on a site adjoining the 1850 building, by Mr B. Guest of Wolverhampton at a cost of £800, to accommodate 120 more worshippers than the old chapel. It was demolished soon after the congregation joined with Trinity in 1964.

The old Methodist chapel in Rookery Street in about 1920. This was built in 1825 and was the first offshoot of the Wolverhampton Darlington Street Methodist Circuit. It was used as a chapel until the opening of Trinity in 1887, then used as a school building.

R&S Carpet Warehouse, Rookery Street in 1984, the same building as the Methodist chapel above. From about 1912 the building housed the Electric Theatre which became the Ideal Cinema, known locally as the Smack, in 1931. It was always regarded as a poor relation to the purpose built Regal, and showed its last film in 1957, becoming, briefly, a dance hall in 1962. The building's final use was as a carpet store, burned down in 1991.

Butchers boys, Bert Goodare and Harry Francis Sanders (left), pictured outside Ted Hulme's shop in New Street in the late 1920s. Ted Hulme's father also had a butchers shop which stood in Rookery Street, opposite the Pyle Cock public house. Harry Sanders later went on to work for another Wednesfield butcher, Walter Downing, whose shop was in the High Street, while Bert Goodare went to work for H.H. Walker of Willenhall after leaving Hulme's and later joined the RAF.

No. 18 High Street in about 1934, with Mrs Tyler standing outside. This was opposite the present Glen's fruit shop.

The greengrocers at 7 High Street. On the left is Mrs Adey.

Councillor Arthur Johnson, Chairman of Wednesfield Urban District Council, visiting the new Wednesfield Market which opened on 13 December 1960. The *Wednesfield News* described 'the orderly rows of little stalls with their gaily striped awnings (which) lent an air of bright cheerfulness, an atmosphere of Christmas to the car park opposite the council offices in Alfred Squire Road'. The market moved to its present site in 1970.

Wednesfield Urban District Council Offices in Alfred Squire Road, which were opened on 2 April 1955 in the presence of Jennie Lee MP. Since Wednesfield's merger with Wolverhampton in 1966 the building has been used as a community centre.

The Queen's visit to Wednesfield on 24 May 1962. In this photograph Her Majesty is shaking hands with Mrs Rhys Thomas, wife of the Chairman of Willenhall Urban District Council. Also pictured, in uniform, is the Lord Lieutenant of Staffordshire, Mr H. Wallace Copeland. The Queen had spent the morning in Wolverhampton and was cheered on her way to Walsall by 6,000 schoolchildren lining Lakefield Road.

The Queen's visit to Wednesfield, 24 May 1962. Carol Anne Burns, aged seven, of Pickering Road, a pupil at Neachells Lane Primary School, waits to present a bouquet of pink roses and white lilies. The *Wednesfield News* reported that 'she remained perfectly calm and curtsied most gracefully'.

The Dog and Partridge, one of the oldest inns in Wednesfield, undergoing reconstruction of the upper storey in the early years of this century.

The Dog and Partridge and landlords Mr and Mrs Gregory. Little is known of the history of the building before the Gregory family took over, although it appears on the tithe map of 1843 and is well placed to be a much older coaching inn.

The Dog and Partridge in the 1950s.

Mr and Mrs Gregory with a bowls trophy at the back of the Dog and Partridge. Harry Gregory, who died in 1957 at the age of 89, was a bowler himself and was responsible for the formation of the Staffordshire Crown Green Bowling Association. The green at the Dog and Partridge was one of the oldest in the area.

The Dog and Partridge Bowls Team at around the turn of the century, with their trophies.

The Gregory family of Wednesfield. John Thomas and Mary Ann Gregory sit surrounded by their family, Mary (known as Polly), Harry, Joe and his wife Emmy, Ernie, Florence, Charley, Percy, Kate, Polly, Jack, Evelyn, Ernest, Millard and Bert. The boy at the back left and the man in the cap at the back are unidentified.

The New Crown Bowling Club, Nordley Road in 1947. Pictured in the front row are, from left to right: R. Oakley, F.J. Noble, Mrs R. Oakley, S. Goodyear, Mrs W. Downing, B. Beston (the league secretary), B. Smith and Ray Oakley. Middle row: W. Powell, B. Tomlinson, E. Gorge, J. Guffogg, C. Langley, S. Littlehales, H. Green, P. Terry, Les Littlehales and C. Terry. Back row: K. Smith, H. Palmer, O. Hand, R. Wood, R. Littlehales and T. Knoble.

A Sunday morning outing from the Angel Inn, High Street in the 1920s. Among those pictured are Jim Howe, the licensee, Bill Jackson, George Kitson, Charlie Hubball, Tom Rowley, Bill McConkey, Will Hayes, Dick Spencer, Ernie Bedale, Tom Griffiths, Jack Peers, Jack Froggatt, Ernie Wakelam, Edward (Jack) Hayes and Archie Bartlett. Tom Griffiths had a coach and transport business in Lichfield Road.

Wednesfield Labour Party visiting London on 16 September 1950. Among those pictured are the Griffiths family, the Preece family, Mr Osborne, Bert Hicklin, Ben Wear, Mr and Mrs Hill, Mr and Mrs Phillips, Mr and Mrs Harry Russell, the Pugh family, Mrs L. Bird, Mrs Turley, Mr S. Hayes, Councillor Jack Husbands and his wife, Mrs Vaughan, Stanley Evans MP, Tom Daffern, Stan Norman and his wife, the Broomhall family, Trevor Nicklin, Mr and Mrs Bloor, Councillor Mary Newey and her husband, Mrs Craven, and the Hayward family.

St Thomas' Sunday school teachers in the 1920s. Pictured in the back row, left to right, are Harry Price, Percy Lowe, Fred Griffiths, J.T. Hughes, and Harold Weston. Middle row: Mrs Griffiths, Freda Easthope, Lily Bache, Iris Millington, Myra Smith and Evelyn Challenor. Front row: Dorothy Lewis, Edith Weston, and three not known.

A float for Wednesfield Carnival in Graiseley Lane in about 1929.

The Warren and Day families pictured in Taylor Street in about 1930. From left to right are Tom Warren, -?-, Frank Warren, Howard Day, Sid Day, -?-, -?-, Margaret Saunders and Gordon Day.

Cub Scouts camp at Gailey in the 1920s. Wednesfield Wesleyan chapel started the 2nd Wednesfield troops of Scouts, Guides and Cubs in the early '20s.

Wednesfield Choral Society in the 1920s. Holding the bouquet is Megan Stephenson, the pianist.

Wednesfield Operatic Society performing *The Mikado* in the early 1930s at the Picture House, Rookery Street. Among those pictured are Arthur Ellison, ? Humphries, Bert Done, ? Williams, Mr Walsh and Horace Broadbent. The youth is Harry Donovan Adey and Nankipoo, Donald Waltho.

Wednesfield Football Club in about 1949. Pictured are, back row: Ben Wear, -?-, Denis Bailey, Roy Banks, Bill Joyce, the chairman, Colin Jones, George Habberley, the secretary, Fred Jones, and Arthur Clift, the manager. Seated: ? Withers, -?-, Charles Wright, Bert Benton and Denis Hulme. Front: -?-, Arthur Stanley.

Wednesfield FC at the George V Playing Fields in about 1952.

Wednesfield Church Institute FC in about the 1890s.

Kathleen (Margaret) Saunders examines the sun dial in the rose garden in Wednesfield Park in about 1934. The park was laid out in 1925 and was trebled in size in 1936 with the addition of the George V Playing Field.

The bowling green at Wednesfield Park in about 1934.

The children's paddling pool, Wednesfield Park, in about 1963.

Kathleen (Margaret) Saunders in the cornfield on the site of the present George V Playing Fields in about 1934. The tennis pavilion and St Thomas' church can be seen in the background.

The Neachells public house at the corner of Willenhall Road and Neachells Lane in the 1930s, soon after conversion from a private house called Neachells House.

The Regal Cinema in the mid-1950s from St Thomas' churchyard. The cinema opened on 14 October 1935, part of the Clifton chain run by Captain Clift and Leon Salberg. There were seats for 1,028, and the first manager was Alex Tuck, who had previously managed the Dunstall Cinema and later moved to the Clifton, Fallings Park. The Regal closed on 17 March 1962, showing *The Naked Edge* with Gary Cooper. The last manager was Mr H.J.E. Davies, who had taken over from Alex Tuck twenty-seven years before. Following demolition of the cinema, a supermarket was built on the site.

Wednesfield Board School, Neachells Lane, built in 1895 for 300 children. This school later became Wednesfield Council School and is now part of Neachells Infants' School.

Wednesfield Council School Group 6 pupils in March 1906. The headmaster at this time was Mr Last.

St Thomas' School, Graiseley Lane, built in 1856. Percy Gregory of the Dog and Partridge family is standing by the headmaster. Ada Millichamp, who first went to this school in 1907, describes the children's clothes in her book *Memories of Yesterday*. She says, 'We children had to come straight home from school and change pinafores to one already soiled in order to keep the one clean for school tomorrow. Our warm, lined winter dresses would probably be worn the whole term without being washed.'

St Thomas' School in 1927. Pictured are, back row, left to right: ? Beards, E. Adey, E. Craven, ? Tonks, E. Corbett, V. Colley, R. Bickley, B. Ratcliffe. Second row: W. Lacey, E. Paice, ? Williams, H. Jones, J. Nicholls, J. Taylor, ? Lloyd, ? Cooper, S. Gilbert, A. Jones. Centre row: Miss Lake, M. Swatman, K. Hillett, ? Turner, F. Harley, M. Upton, ? Nicholls, ? Davies, ? Wall, L. Beards, ? Toombs, B. Lewis. Kneeling: Norman Day, ? Badger, ? Dillon, ? Bleasdale, ? Booley, ? Morris, ? Machin, ? Vickers, ? Tomlinson, ? Green. Cross-legged: ? Nicholls, ? Jones, ? Lathe, ? Simmons, ? Ashton, ? Whitehouse, ? Bates, ? Nicholls, ? Barnes.

Wednesfield Kindergarten, 54 Graiseley Lane in about 1932. Pictured in the back row: ? Kirk, Margaret Saunders, Stella Thompson, Sidney Davis, Sybil Tonks. On the bench: ? Kirk, Betty Powell, Freddie Ellard, Bessie Ketland and Tony Downing. The two at the front are unidentified.

The Temperance Hall, Hall Street in about 1960 when it was used as the Brockhouse greasing bay. In 1864 this hall was used as a school by one Emma Wootton. In 1872 it was used for entertainments, with a mesmerist appearing for three weeks.

Weldless Steel Tube Co., which employed about 600 men in 1914, but suspended work from 1931 to 1934 due to the Depression.

Apprentices undergoing their first nine months of training at the special apprentice workshop at Weldless Steel Tube in the mid-1960s.

Weldless Steel Tube Co. apprentices making a model of a 350 ton hydraulic press in about 1963.

Weldless Steel Tube Apprentices' Association members setting off for a weekend caving expedition in the mid-1960s.

Trapmakers at Henry Lane, Hickman Street in about 1912. Left to right are Bill Bradley of Hickman Street, Thomas White of Graiseley Lane, whose family had been trapmakers since 1818, Frank Mason of Rookery Street, and Albert Jones of the Rickyard, who was killed in Flanders in 1915.

George Jones, trapmaker, pictured in 1980. He worked at Marshalls of Lichfield Road from 1911 to 1968. His collection of traps is used by local historian John Smallshire.

Making castings at C. & B. Smith, Neachells Lane in about 1963. Originally founded in 1909 in Bloomsbury Street, Wolverhampton, the foundry at Wednesfield opened in the 1950s to make clutch housings and gearboxes. It closed at the end of 1985 during the recession in the British motor industry.

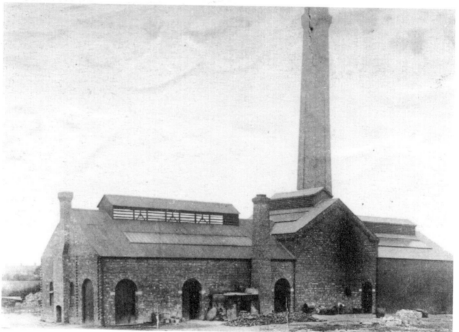

Wednesfield Phosphorus Works in October 1893. This was situated on the Bentley Canal.

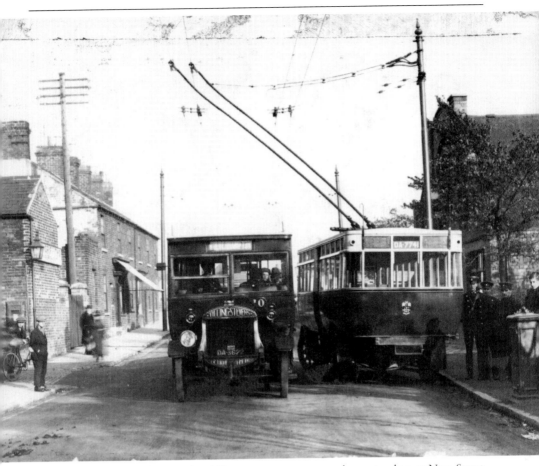

The No. 1 trolleybus showing its ability to manoeuvre round a motor bus at New Street, Wednesfield in 1923. This was the first trolleybus route inaugurated by Wolverhampton Corporation Transport, replacing the trams. On the right is the old tram terminus, which continued to be used by the trolleybuses until the widening of the Rookery Street canal bridge, and on the left is the premises of John Griffiths, iron merchant.

The No. 2 trolleybus at New Cross on its way from Wednesfield to Wolverhampton. The Wednesfield route was only able to use single-decker vehicles because of the difficulties posed by the railway bridge at the lower end of Broad Street, Wolverhampton.

SECTION TWO
Around Wednesfield

Wood End Road, looking towards the Castle Inn, in about 1910.

Bellamy Lane in 1954. The cast iron window frames of these houses were typical of those throughout the industrial Black Country. The houses have now been demolished.

The Old Vine Inn, Lichfield Road, looking out from the village. The Vine has since been rebuilt and all the other buildings have disappeared.

Lichfield Road, looking towards Castle Bridge in 1959. Note the trolleybus poles and wires.

Broad Lane North, looking towards Perry Hall canal bridge in 1960.

March End Road in about 1930.

Perry Hall Bridge in July 1960.

Ridge Lane at the junction with Moathouse Lane in the 1960s. The group of four houses on the right are shown on the tithe map of the 1840s as belonging to Sarah Meredith.

Moathouse Lane Shopping Centre, built to serve the Moathouse Estate which was one of the first of the Wolverhampton overspill housing estates. Its name was taken from the Moathouse Farm which was originally near Moathouse Bridge but was later rebuilt around 1860 near the Lichfield Road and known locally as Hyde's Farm. Roads on the Moathouse Estate were named after Wednesfield councillors of the '50s and '60s.

Devils Elbow Lane in 1959 and, below, the canal bridge in about 1985. In the 1960s residents campaigned to have the name changed to Kennedy Avenue, after John F. Kennedy. Part of the road was actually renamed Whitehouse Avenue, after a large house in the neighbourhood, but the section closest to the canal remains Devils Elbow Lane. One of Devils Elbow Cottages can just be seen in the top picture. They were demolished soon afterwards.

Long Knowle Lane in 1929.

The corner of Wood Hayes and Blackhalve Lane in about 1930.

Shopping centres at Long Knowle Lane, above, and Fairview Road, D'Eyncourt, below, in the 1960s. All the new housing estates were supplied with similar blocks of shops with flats above. Long Knowle Estate was named after Long Knowle Farm which stood in the vicinity of Bradburn Road.

Ashmore Cottage, off Blackhalve Lane, demolished in 1954. This was typical of the miners' cottages, built by the miners themselves, which were dotted around the mining area to the east of Wednesfield as well as the rest of the Black Country. Collieries in the vicinity included those at Coppice, Ashmore Park, Pool Hayes and Castle Bridge.

Linthouse Lane in February 1960, above, and, below, in about 1950. These pictures show that there was very little development in this area before the building of Ashmore Park.

Ashmore Park Shopping Centre in the mid-1960s. In the lower picture the remains of the Ashmore moat can just be seen on the right. In 1666 this was the site of an eight hearth hall belonging to Robert Leveson, later replaced with a more modest farm building which remained for a short while after the building of the estate.

Millbank Street, Ashmore Park in 1961. The Ashmore Park Estate was built from 1951 as an area of housing overspill for Wolverhampton, with a target of 6,600 new homes in Ashmore Park, Long Knowle, Linthouse, Moathouse, Stubby Lane and Prestwood Road.

Wood End Methodist church, pictured in 1982 shortly before demolition. The church was opened in 1860 and was associated originally with the Willenhall Circuit rather than the neighbouring Wednesfield. However, it was one of the churches that joined together to form the new Wednesfield Methodist church which was built on its site and opened in 1983.

John Mattox and Sons' key factory, Amos Lane. Although Willenhall is the acknowledged centre for lock making, both Wolverhampton and Wednesfield had many lock and keymakers in the nineteenth century. Keymakers called Mattox first appear in the trade directories in the 1850s. The factory, which was built in the 1870s and extended in about 1900, still trades under the name of John Mattox, but is run by the Hughes brothers who produce specialized keys to fit old doors in buildings such as churches and embassies.

St Thomas' Infants' School, Wood End Road opened in July 1876 as the Wood End National School and could accommodate 150 children. It was later known as Wood End Infants' School.

Wood End Infants' School in the mid-1920s.

The girls' cottages at the Cottage Homes in about 1900. The cottage homes were built by the Wolverhampton Board of Guardians in 1889 at a cost of about £20,000. They provided places for 240 children who would otherwise have been accommodated in the Wolverhampton Union workhouse then in Bilston Road. The children were not orphans but those whose parents had fallen on hard times and were unable to support them. Some of the parents were themselves in the workhouse or in gaol. Some children had frequent stays in the Cottage Homes, returning to their own homes in between, presumably when times were better.

The entrance to the Cottage Homes. The buildings covered twenty acres and included an infirmary, schools and workshops.

The Cottage Homes schools in about 1900

The bakery at the Cottage Homes in about 1900. The children were all taught skills of various kinds so that they could support themselves when they left. Those who left in their early teens were generally found employment and were helped if their first position was not successful.

The carpenters shop at the Cottage Homes in about 1900.

The tailors shop at the Cottage Homes in about 1900.

The girls' sewing room at the Cottage Homes in about 1900. Mrs A. Barrett, the matron, is standing next to the cupboard. The girls were all taught domestic skills and many were put into service when they were old enough to leave the homes.

The Cottage Homes school in about 1900. The school closed in 1932 when it was felt that the children would benefit from mixing with other children. They were sent to various local schools.

The Cottage Homes infants' school in about 1900. The class glimpsed through the door is standing on the steps of the gallery while doing their lessons.

Christmas at the Cottage Homes in 1936. The Cottage Homes gradually changed their role to become a local authority children's home. During the 1960s the policy was to provide smaller homes run on family lines in different parts of the town, and by the end of the decade the Cottage Homes were no longer needed. Braybrook House Assessment Centre was opened on the site by Princess Margaret in 1974. All the original buildings have now been demolished.

The Castle Inn, Wood End, listed in a trade directory of 1888 with Sarah Harper as the landlady. The inn, however, is obviously much older in origin, appearing on a survey of lands of the Duke of Sutherland in 1764. The piece of land opposite is called Moat Croft, suggesting some kind of fortified building in the area.

The Pheasant Inn, Long Knowle. In the early part of the last century this pub was owned by the Mason family, two of whom are said to have been hanged for theft from churches and the houses of the gentry in the Shropshire countryside. The old pub was pulled down in the 1930s and replaced by a new building.

The old Vine Inn, Lichfield Road in the 1930s. Fred and Florence Cocking, the licensees, were the parents of Mrs Florence Lathe who only recently retired from the pub, having been born there in 1928. It was previously known as the 'Young and Old' because of the age difference between Floss Cocking and her first husband Tom Powell.

The Pear Tree Inn, Cannock Road, one of the oldest in Wednesfield, before rebuilding in about 1950.

Licensees Mr and Mrs Bert Adey outside the Pear Tree Inn in a coach belonging to Bertram Mills' Circus in 1931, the year they took over the license. Mr and Mrs Adey left the Pear Tree in 1970 when Bert was aged 72.

Bert Adey, well-known local boxer and licensee of the Pear Tree Inn, pictured in 1920, the year after he had taken part in one of Britain's last twenty-round contests. He had his first professional contest in 1913 at the age of 16 and took part in about 100 bouts during his professional career, winning 85. In 1930 he took out a promoter's licence and organized fights at the Riding School, Newhampton Road, Cleveland Road Stadium, Wednesfield Drill Hall and at the Pear Tree. He also managed local boxers such as Fred Lowbridge, Bonny Evans and Fred Blything.

The Southern Area Featherweight Championship boxing match between Tommy Rogers and Tommy Hyams at the Pear Tree Inn, Cannock Road, 7 August 1933. Landlord Bert Adey promoted regular boxing matches at the pub.

SECTION THREE

Heath Town

Wednesfield Road, with the junction of Railway Street on the left in about 1905. The building with the lamp on the right is the Star Hotel. The single-deck tram is running on the Lorain system, which was introduced into Wolverhampton in 1902. The section to Deans Road was constructed early in 1903 and extended to New Street, Wednesfield in 1904.

Wednesfield Road looking towards Wednesfield after the introduction of overhead wires for the trams in 1921. The Congregational church can just be seen on the left, and the junction with Heath Street is on the right.

Wednesfield Road showing the boundary between Wolverhampton and Heath Town in 1921. St Barnabas' church and the adjoining row of shops are now all that remain of the old Heath Town.

Wednesfield Road in 1955, looking towards the junction with Grove Street, the Congregational church and Wolverhampton. Houses similar to these abounded in Heath Town but were demolished in the early 1960s.

Two views of Wolverhampton Road, the top one taken in August 1905, and the other probably at about the same date. On the left of both pictures is the Congregational church and the Talbot Inn, which is having barrels of beer delivered in the lower picture. The large house is on the junction with Woden Road.

Wolverhampton Road in September (above) and January (below) 1962, as demolition was beginning. In the top photograph the Heath Town Wesleyan Methodist church can be seen on the corner of Dean Street, and the junction of Hill Street is on the left. Below is the section between Hill Street and Tudor Road, looking towards Wolverhampton. Miss D. Eatwell's Hardware store is on the right in the foreground.

The back of Wolverhampton Road near the junction of Deans Road in the 1950s. The very poor housing conditions in this area are clearly shown in this photograph of the communal yard containing privies and outhouses. The chimney belonged to the Midland Industries factory.

Wednesfield Road in more recent times, looking towards Wolverhampton town centre. Both Chubb's new factory on Wednesfield Road, next to St Barnabas' church, and their old works in Wolverhampton can be seen in the photograph. Also shown are the older council housing of the Burton Road Estate, St Peter's church and the Mander tower.

The new flats near the junction of Woden Road in the late 1960s. Wolverhampton town centre, including the Tarmac office block, can be seen in the background.

Railway Street in June 1962, showing the unusual curved terrace of houses at the junction with Wolverhampton Road.

Grove Street in 1955, from under the railway bridge looking towards Wolverhampton Road.

Back houses in Grove Street which had a number of courts off it until its demolition in the 1960s.

Woden Road, showing the boundary between Wolverhampton and Heath Town in 1921. Woden Road was originally two separate roads known as James Street at the Wednesfield Road end and Spring Valley Street at the Cannock Road end. Woden Road School was built at the junction, making it into one road.

Willenhall Road, showing the boundary between Wolverhampton and Heath Town in 1921. The Royal Oak public house can be seen on the left of the photograph.

The boundary between Wednesfield and Heath Town, running through the grounds of New Cross workhouse, pictured in October 1921.

Holy Trinity church, built in 1850. John Moor Paget, the local landowner, donated the land for church and vicarage and an appeal for funds was made. Henry Rogers made a donation of £1000 and was selected to lay the foundation stone on 4 June. Edward Banks was the architect of the church, which opened in 1852.

The interior of Holy Trinity church, built in the Victorian Gothic style.

St Barnabas' church, Wednesfield Road, built in 1892.

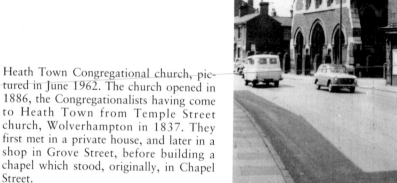

Heath Town Congregational church, pictured in June 1962. The church opened in 1886, the Congregationalists having come to Heath Town from Temple Street church, Wolverhampton in 1837. They first met in a private house, and later in a shop in Grove Street, before building a chapel which stood, originally, in Chapel Street.

Heath Town Wesleyan Methodist church, pictured in June 1962, the year of its closure before demolition. The church was built in 1859 and opened for worship in March 1860 by Revd S. D. Waddy, President of the Wesleyan Conference. It was designed by well-known local architect George Bidlake, and the *Wolverhampton Chronicle* commented that it reflected 'great credit upon both architect and builder'.

Cross Street, pictured in June 1962, with the old Primitive Methodist chapel, opened in 1848. Little is known of the history of this chapel, which was clearly in industrial use by this time.

Charles Hales' butchers shop, 54 Wolverhampton Road, at Christmas 1931. The Hales family business was at Cannock market, although they also had a shop in Dudley Road, Wolverhampton. Charles, however, set up on his own account in Heath Town, and is clearly proud of his array of different birds and meats available for the festive season.

Heath Town Park, which was leased by the Heath Town Urban District Council from the Ecclesiastical Commissioners in 1917, before being bought outright for £750 in 1920. It is believed that the land had previously been rough colliery ground and there is a clause in the original lease indemnifying the Ecclesiastical Commissioners against claims in respect of damage due to old mine workings.

The Fever Hospital at Heath Town, built in 1894, was initially for smallpox patients, but later used for other infectious diseases such as scarlet fever. Situated in isolation at Bowmans Harbour, the hospital was reached by a cart track from Deans Road bridge.

New Cross Hospital pictured in 1974. This was originally built as the Wolverhampton Union workhouse, replacing the old workhouse on Bilston Road in 1901. The workhouse system was abolished in 1930, by which time New Cross's hospital function had already superseded that of the workhouse, although an institution and casual ward for tramps, known as the Spike, was maintained until the 1960s. The architect of New Cross was Arthur Marshall, who also designed Darlington Street Methodist church in Wolverhampton.

Heath Town Baths and Library pictured in 1983. This building was opened in December 1932 and originally included a main swimming bath, a children's swimming bath, a public wash house for hand and machine washing, and a branch library and reading room. The opening of the library was the cause of some controversy, when it was proposed to appoint a female librarian in charge, the main point at issue being high male unemployment at the time.

The Star Hotel, Wolverhampton Road, pictured shortly before demolition in the 1960s. This pub stood at the corner of Cross Street.

A children's Christmas party at the Star Hotel in 1952.

The Swan Inn, 213 Wolverhampton Road, pictured in 1953. Landlord James Joyce is standing in the doorway, looking very proud of his window boxes and hanging baskets. This pub, which stood at the corner of Church Street, was demolished in 1961.

A children's outing from the Swan Inn to Cannock Chase in 1950.

The old Travellers Rest, Wolverhampton Road, shortly before demolition in September 1962. This pub was later rebuilt at the junction with Woden Road.

The Bulls Head, Wednesfield Road in May 1961. This is one of the few old public houses in Heath Town to escape demolition during the redevelopment of the early 1960s. At that time it was owned by Joules Brewery of Stone, Staffordshire.

The Cock Inn, Church Street, at the junction with Tudor Road, in May 1961, shortly before demolition. This was one of three pubs in the short length of Church Street in the 1860s.

The Forge Hammer, Heath Street, shortly before demolition in June 1962.

The General Havelock, Alma Street in 1962. The name of Alma Street commemorates the Crimean War battle of 1854, while General Havelock was a hero of the Indian Mutiny who died in India in 1857.

A children's Christmas party at the Squirrel Inn, Bushbury Road in 1951. This pub was demolished in the 1960s and a new pub, the Great Horse, built on the site.

The old and new Victoria Inn, Deans Road, pictured in around 1940, before demolition of the old building and after its replacement with a brand new pub.

A VE Day street party in Alma Street on 8 May 1945. Causeway Lake School can be seen on the left of the picture and Green's shop in the centre. Playing the piano on the right of the picture is Billy Blower, and among the children pictured in the front row are Mel Jones, Margaret Jones, Frank Hammond, ? Harrison, Bobby Hammond, Joan Hammond and ? Davies. Among the adults in the back row are Mrs Wall, third from left, Mrs Harrison, near the shop doorway, Doris Cooper, holding the baby, and the man near the house window is Joey Howell.

Princess Margaret at Heath Town on 1 April 1969. During the course of her visit she called on Mr and Mrs Ray Finnerty in their maisonette in Hobgate Road, chosen as 'typical of the people living on the estate'. It was also planned for the princess to visit two families on the twenty-first floor of Alder House but on the day a power cut put the lifts out of action and there was some panic until power was restored only five minutes before the royal party arrived.

Woden Road School was built by the joint Heath Town and Wednesfield School Board in 1898 to accommodate 400 children. The headmaster in 1900 was Mr Hallam and the infants school mistress was Miss Povey. The buildings are currently occupied by St Stephen's Church of England Primary School.

Causeway Lake School, Alma Street, was built in 1897 to replace an older building which housed Causeway Lake Church School. The new buildings were paid for by subscription and the school was a branch of St James' School, Horseley Fields, being in the parish of St James' Wolverhampton. In 1900 it was a mixed and infants school catering for 400 children.

Holy Trinity School, Heath Town, pictured in October 1962. The school was built in 1854 for 450 children but failed to gain much of a reputation until the arrival of Elizabeth Saunders in 1882 when it became more successful. A new school was built in the early 1970s. The old building had been described as 'structurally the worst school in the town' in 1948. Nevertheless, it continued to be used as an annexe until a fire in 1985. After that the building was allowed to deteriorate until it was finally demolished.

The demolition of Heath Town Wesleyan Methodist School, Dean Street in December 1964. The school was built in 1866 for 340 children.

Zachariah and Ernest Pursehouse, coal and lime merchants of New Cross Wharf, in 1923.
New Cross workhouse is in the background.

The junction of the Wyrley and Essington and Bentley Canals at New Cross in about 1920. The Bentley Canal linked the Wyrley and Essington with the Birmingham Canal Navigation's Anson branch near Walsall, following the amalgamation of the two companies in 1840.

The Bentley Canal at New Cross locks in 1970. This canal, which was less than four miles long, opened in 1843 and was largely abandoned in 1961.

Wednesfield Heath station, the original Wolverhampton station, as the Grand Junction Railway line did not go into the town centre at that time. The station was opened in July 1837 and the first train to arrive from Birmingham, making the journey in 35 minutes at a passenger fare of 1s 6d in an open carriage or 2s 6d in a closed carriage, was the 'Wildfire'. Passenger services to the station were withdrawn in 1873, but the line continued to be used as the Wolverhampton to Walsall link until 1965.

SECTION FOUR

Springfield, Park Village & Fallings Park

Culwell Street, Springfield in the 1950s. The Springfield Estate was planned by Wolverhampton Council to rehouse people who were being displaced from the town centre under the Artisans' Dwellings scheme of the 1870s. However, after the council had purchased the land, no developer could be found to build the 290 planned houses, and the estate had to be sold off piecemeal. By 1880 only 75 houses had been built.

Bagnall Street in 1955. The Culwell Tavern can be seen in the top picture, its name taken from the Cul Well, a spring formerly to be seen at the junction of Wednesfield Road and Bridge Street.

The corner of Field Street and Hilton Street in 1955, with its typical corner shop.

Bailey Street in February 1963. These fairly substantial houses, which faced the high level railway line, were demolished soon afterwards and their site now forms part of the Great Western pub's garden and car park.

Grimstone Street, looking towards Springfield Brewery, in 1955.

Junction Street, looking towards Field Street, in the 1950s. All these houses, speculatively built in the 1880s after Wolverhampton's failed first attempt at town planning, were in poor condition by the late 1950s and were demolished soon afterwards.

The Coach and Horses, Cannock Road at the turn of the century. Standing next to Grimstone Farm, which can be seen on the left, this may have been a private house, and appears to have been converted into a pub by Samuel Wright, formerly landlord of the neighbouring Wagon and Horses, in the early 1870s.

The service to commemorate the start of building of St Stephens church, 8 September 1907. The first sod was cut by Mrs Collett, wife of the vicar of St Mary's.

Shri Guru Ravidas Temple, Horseley Fields, pictured in December 1977. This was formerly Mount Zion Methodist church, which was built in 1865-7, replacing an earlier chapel on the site. As well as being a thriving church, with a number of prominent individuals in membership, it was one of the first to provide educational classes for its adult members. The Methodist church closed in 1968 and, after its use as a temple, was demolished in the late '70s.

(Opposite) St Stephen's School, Grimstone Street in March 1964. This originally opened on 13 September 1879 and continued as a school until the mid-1970s. It reopened as the Springfield Community Centre on 13 September 1979. St Stephen's School now uses the buildings which were formerly Springfield Secondary School, Springfield Road.

A street party for the coronation of King George VI in Field Street in 1937.

A.E. Beresford, wholesale grocer of Union Mill Street, and his employees. This warehouse originally belonged to James Shipton, canal carriers, and may have been built by Shipton in the 1830s. It still exists, and the canal loading doors and other evidence of its former function can still be seen.

Foden steam wagons belonging to J.N. Miller pictured at the Old Steam Mill in about 1920. Miller's started off as Nortons' towards the end of the eighteenth century, but their old wooden mill was destroyed by fire in 1851 and replaced by a new brick building which has been much added to over the years, although the original structure, with many of its original features, can still be seen. The mill had its own canal basin, and water transport continued to be important for its raw materials. Miller's closed down recently and the mill buildings are currently being subdivided and sold off.

Edmund Vaughan Stampings, Horseley Fields, pictured early this century. The firm, which was about 140 years old, closed down in 1980 and the foundry has now been subdivided into workshop units.

Springfield Brewery, showing the ornate entrance, in April 1974. The brewery was opened by William Butler & Co. in 1873, replacing their old premises at Priestfield, and only ceased brewing in 1991. The entrance gateway is a listed structure.

Springfield Brewery from the railway in 1899, showing the range of new buildings which had been erected around the original brewhouse during the 1880s.

Butler's Brewery Cooperage in 1952

Women workers at Butler's Brewery Maltings in 1918. Note the traditional malt shovel and rake held by the women at either end.

Butler's Brewery workers in about 1910. In the centre of the back row is Dick Birch, while Bill Birch is second from right, holding the bottle, in the second row. The Birch family was associated with the brewery for a long time.

Butler's Brewery Fire Brigade in about 1900. Pictured are T. Price, J. Willis, H. Birch, H. Turner, ? Cooper, T. Ambrose, G. Shelley, T. Appleby and A. Rendison.

Butler's Brewery dray horses, Gilbert and Nobby, pictured in 1952 with W. Hayward and A. Evans.

Butler's Brewery football team in about 1927.

The unveiling of the Second World War addition to Butler's Brewery war memorial by Revd Percy Bourne, vicar of St Stephen's, on 16 September 1949. Eleven brewery employees were killed between 1939 and 1945. The memorial, which originally stood in the brewery yard, is now at the sports and social club in Springfield Road.

Cannock Road in May 1929, looking through the railway bridge by Woden Road towards Fallings Park.

Cannock Road, showing the boundary between Wolverhampton and Heath Town in October 1921. The shop in the foreground on the left was that of J. Overton, boot repairer, and at the other end of the row of houses was the Nine Elm Stores, at the junction of Nine Elms Lane, run by F. Andrews and bearing the slogan 'which surpasses all others'.

Cannock Road from the opposite direction in 1921.

Bridge Street, near the junction with Wood Street, in May 1973.

Bank Street in May 1973, looking towards Chubb's Park Lane factory.

A street party in Park Village to celebrate VE Day in 1945.

Stratton Street Methodist church in 1906, just as the building was being finished. There had originally been a Primitive Methodist chapel in Culwell Street but when this building was condemned it was decided to move to a new site in the expanding Park Village area.

The Clifton Cinema, Fallings Park, pictured in February 1962, a month before its demolition. This was the last cinema to open in Wolverhampton, in 1938, and lasted for only twenty-three years. It was owned by Captain Sidney Clift and the first manager was Alex Tuck, who moved from the Regal at Wednesfield. The last film shown in November 1961 was *Can Can*. A large supermarket now occupies the site.

A fire at Wearwell Cycles on 4 March 1932. The Wearwell Cycle factory was in Colliery Road at this time, off Willenhall Road, having been started by Jack, Henry and George Clarke in the 1890s in Darlington Street. The firm continued until the 1980s, though not, by that time, in Wolverhampton.

The exterior of the Efandem Battery works, Park Lane in 1922. The firm was later taken over by Ever Ready but the Park Lane factory closed in 1980.

Women labelling flat torch batteries at Efandem in 1922. Production of this battery type moved to one of Ever Ready's south-eastern factories after the Second World War, but was restarted at Park Lane in 1970.

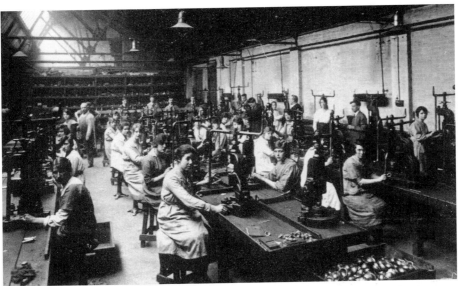

Working at Efandem in 1922. The women in this workshop were making mild steel reflector housings for cycle lamps, which continued to be made at the factory until 1976. Finished examples can be seen in the box at the front of the photograph.

Lorries outside Guy Motors works in Park Lane in 1925. Guy was started in 1914 by Sydney Guy, who had previously worked at Sunbeam, and continued until the 1970s as part of British Leyland. The firm mainly made commercial vehicles, lorries and buses, but also made cars in the early days.

Cars and lorries lined up inside Guy Motors works in April 1925.

Operating machinery at Guy Motors during the Second World War. Women workers had not previously been employed in the factory

Attracting women workers to Guy Motors during the Second World War. The firm made history in recruiting part-time workers for the first time.

Full-time women workers at Guy Motors during the Second World War, taken from a brochure designed to recruit women to the factory. One example quoted is a mother of eleven children, seven under 14, who worked 55 hours per week at the factory and on Sundays 'cooks, washes, cleans and mends for her husband and family'.

Blakemore's Fallings Park Stores in the 1920s. Blakemore's was established in 1867 and formed a chain of grocery stores plus a wholesale business in Wolverhampton.

Fallings Park Garden Suburb, established by Sir Richard Paget, who owned the Old Fallings Estate, on the model of such developments as Hampstead Garden Suburb and Welwyn Garden City. The first six houses were started in 1907 and a Model Housing Exhibition opened in September 1908, including a number of other houses built in competition by architects from the local area and elsewhere. Although the scheme included seventy-five houses by 1915, it was never fully completed, and the originally tenanted and centrally managed houses were being sold off by the 1920s.

The visit of Sir George Chubb to the Fallings Park Model Housing in July 1908, when the foundation stone of the new Chubb works was also laid. Chubb's were interested in the provision of suitable housing for their expanding workforce. Some of the houses were still unfinished and can be seen in the background.

Fallings Park Methodist Church in the 1930s, soon after its opening in 1936. There had been a church at Fallings Park since 1908, as part of the Garden Suburb scheme, but this was originally a wooden building.

Judging the babies at the August Fete at Fallings Park in 1908.

Newbolds Farm in 1909. Built in the eighteenth century, this continued to be a working farmhouse until 1933, and still exists although now divided into flats. There had been a farm at Newbolds since at least the twelfth century.

Farmer James Cope at Newbolds Farm, the last person to farm the land here.

Moving in to Fallings Park Fire Station in September 1960. The fire station, which cost about £50,000, was built to serve the northern part of the town and included a district fire station, auxiliary fire service garage and ambulance station. The first station officer was W.E. Gibbs and the original brigade came from Wergs Road, Tettenhall, leaving that station to be taken over by Staffordshire.

The junction of Cannock Road and Old Fallings Lane in the 1960s. The roof of the fire station can be seen in the foreground, and the Fine Fare supermarket occupies the former site of the Clifton Cinema. Bushbury Hill can be seen in the background.

Acknowledgements

All the photographs in this volume are from the collection of Wolverhampton Public Libraries. The authors are most grateful to all those who have donated photographs to the collection, either in the past or specifically for this book, and given permission for their use.

The help of the following in donating pictures and providing information is particularly acknowledged:

Mr J.L. Smallshire, Miss K.M. Saunders, Mr A.H. Chatwin, Mr H.R. Rhodes, Mrs P. Malone, Mr Stride, Ned Williams, Mr Stan Hayes, Mr J.A. Richards, Mr P. Eisenhofer, Miss Freda Easthope, Mrs Iris Millington, Mr Norman Day, Mr Pursehouse, Mrs Florence Lathe, Mr Bert Goodare, Stephen Beardsmore.